ONE Baby For The World

24 Days Of Advent

From A Missions Perspective

BY SHARI TVRDIK

Cup of COLD WATER MINISTRIES

© Cup Of Cold Water Ministries

This book has been published by Cup of Cold Water Ministries. All rights reserved.

100% of the proceeds from this book go CCWM's Global Growth Fund.

Cup of Cold Water Ministries is a 501c3 not for profit Missions Sending organization
Helping people go where God has called them to serve.

Want to talk missions?

Contact us today.

director@ccwm.org

CCWM
P.O. Box 318 Newark, IL 60541 www.ccwm.org

ccwm.org

To Dad, for giving me my love for the true and beautiful story of Christmas, the one that changed my life, the one that changes the world and for showing me the best glimpse possible of the Father's love.

Welcome To Advent

This Christmas, follow the story of Advent over the next 24 days and celebrate what the Lord may speak to you through this by participating in the ***Engage section*** below each advent. You are invited to enjoy our One Baby For The World play list on Spotify by visiting ccwm.org/advent and following the links provided to discover the song connected to each day.

December 1st	*Dark*	page 6
December 2nd	*Interrupted*	page 10
December 3rd	*Overshadowed*	page 16
December 4th	*Infallible*	page 20
December 5th	*Passionate*	page 25
December 6th	*Believers*	page 29
December 7th	*Noticed*	page 33
December 8th	*Loosed*	page 39
December 9th	*Realization*	page 44
December 10th	*Tender*	page 48
December 11th	*Certain*	page 52
December 12th	*Awake*	page 56
December 13th	*Bethlehem*	page 61
December 14th	*Down*	page 66
December 15th	*Small*	page 70
December 16th	*Awe*	page 74
December 17th	*You*	page 78
December 18th	*Glory*	page 84
December 19th	*Found*	page 87
December 20th	*Tell*	page 91
December 21st	*Ordinary*	page 87
December 22nd	*Seek*	page 97
December 23rd	*Gifts*	page 103
December 24th	*Keeper*	page 108

PROLOGUE

When I was a small girl, *long before missions was a part of my life,* I was introduced to Advent through my father's handmade nativity barn created out of left over cedar wood from his shop. It was larger than any nativity I had seen before and didn't look the shape of the usual barns that housed Mary and Joseph. *"But it's square"* I critiqued. My father gently smiled and said, *"It's okay if it doesn't look like what you think it should, it's who lies inside that really matters....**one baby for the entire world.**"*

That stayed with me, settling deep down in my heart. There was one baby, that's it. Nothing else to save us, nothing else to redeem our lives, but one small baby.

Over the years, I've seen the effect of that baby who lived and died and has now come to dwell in countless followers around this globe. He changes everything. He turns the tide, rewrites our story and makes all things new.

The days leading us through Advent are pregnant with meaning when we consider there was no plan B for God. This was the plan, all along.

"Merry Christmas" is a victory shout that leads the way to *"It. Is. Finished."*

It is my hope that you follow along with me on my missionary journey to Mongolia through *One Baby For The World,* and you fully engage with the story of Advent leading you to this Christmas day, and our own victory shout as you embrace the one Baby who came to rescue you.

~Shari Tvrdik

Dark
December 1st

Reading

Isaiah 9:6-7

*For a child is born to us, a son is given to us. The government will rest on his shoulders.
And he will be called: Wonderful Counselor, Mighty God, Everlasting Father, Prince of Peace.
His government and its peace will never end.
He will rule with fairness and justice from the throne of his ancestor David for all eternity.
The passionate commitment of the Lord of Heaven's Armies will make this happen.*

I t was dark.
The world was dark. The people felt it. They understood darkness. Dark governments, dark families, dark hearts. The words of Isaiah fell as a hope to the burdened listeners. Dark eyes staring back at the prophet. Oh, how they needed a Counselor, a Mighty God to free them. Oh, how the broken home needed a Father who would never leave. Peace, Israel needed peace, *of course they did.* But an everlasting peace sounded like a fairy tale. Imagine a government that was fair and just. Heads shake at the idea. That will never happen *or so they thought.* Yet the old prophet was certain, *peering far away into the future* to a time no one else could see. To Israel the words were more like a hopeful dream. They could only wait and observe if Isaiah's words were prophetic predictions, or ramblings of a crazed lunatic.

Thousands of years later, I enter a cold dark tent like home called a ger. *I'm in Mongolia and this is my first week on the mission field.* Inside, I find no fire even though the temperature outside falls far below freezing. I am here on a family visit but in this home, I see no adult, only two small babies no more than weeks old. I spot them side by side all bundled up in thick quilts with tiny round faces peeking out. I watch their breathing as the air is so cold their little breath creates small puffs of steam making it possible for me to see they are living. I am here with the poorest of the poor, perhaps for the very first time of my life. I have entered in.

I rest my heavy backpack on the floor and wait. Moments later, the mother opens the only door in the circular one room house and with her the icy cold air blasts in. She is not dressed for the weather and I notice her small hands red and cracked from cold, wrapped around the handle of a bucket full of wood. She looks empty, desperate, void of hope.

"*I am trying to keep us alive.*" she says, skipping small talk and greetings all together.

I had to choose between wood to keep us warm or rice to eat. I chose wood".

Her eyes told me she was hoping she chose correctly, and then she said, "*Starving is less painful than freezing.*"

Her words break through any remaining boundary I had between myself and the suffering poor. I have exposed myself to the unforgettably forgotten. My heart leaps. I remember what was making my backpack so heavy. I think back to earlier, before I left for this visit, that small voice nudging me to grab the bag of rice sitting on my pantry shelf...*I may need it.* I watch her start the fire in the small wood stove.

Like the prophet, I have a message of hope for her future.

Will she receive it or is it too dark for her to see?

It is indeed dark right now, and darkness is all this mother knows. It is all she believes is possible for her and her babies. I watch her blow on the embers in the wood and think, do you need a counselor mother? Are you seeking Peace? Do you long for A father who provides, protects, loves? Do you need justice mother? Do you ache for fairness?

It doesn't have to stay dark.

The fire ignites, causing an orange glow to reflect off her face. I give her the rice and tell her about Who instructed me to bring it.

Engage

Look for one person in darkness in the next 24 hours. When you find them, show them there is hope using actions alone, not words.

Interrupted
December 2nd

Reading

Malachi 4:5-6

Look, I am sending you the prophet Elijah before the great and dreadful day of the Lord arrives. His preaching will turn the hearts of fathers to their children, and the hearts of children to their fathers. Otherwise I will come and strike the land with a curse.

Luke 1:5-25

When Herod was king of Judea, there was a Jewish priest named Zechariah. He was a member of the priestly order of Abijiah, and his wife, Elizabeth, was from the priestly line of

Aaron. Zechariah and Elizabeth were righteous in God's eyes careful to obey all of the Lord's commandments and regulations. They had no children because Elizabeth was unable to conceive, and they were both very old. One day Zechariah was serving God in the Temple, for his order was on duty that week. As was the custom of the priests, he was chosen by lot to enter the sanctuary of the Lord and burn incense. While the incense was being burned, a great crowd stood outside, praying. While Zechariah was in the sanctuary, an angel of the Lord appeared to him, standing to the right of the incense altar. Zechariah was shaken and overwhelmed with fear when he saw him.

But the angel said,

"Don't be afraid, Zechariah! God has heard your prayer. Your wife, Elizabeth, will give you a son, and you are to name him John. You will have great joy and gladness, and many will rejoice at his birth, for he will be great in the eyes of the Lord. He must never touch wine or other alcoholic drinks. He will be filled with the Holy Spirit, even before his birth. And he will turn many Israelites to the Lord their God. He will be a man with the spirit and power of Elijah. He will prepare the people for the coming of the Lord. He will turn the hearts of the fathers to their children, and he will cause those who are rebellious to accept the wisdom of the godly."

Zechariah said to the angel,

"How can I be sure this will happen? I'm an old man now,

and my wife is also well along in years."
Then the angel said,
"I am Gabriel! I stand in the very presence of God. It was he who sent me to bring you this good news! But now, since you didn't believe what I said, you will be silent and unable to speak until the child is born. For my words will certainly be fulfilled at the proper time."

Meanwhile, the people were waiting for Zechariah to come out of the sanctuary, wondering why he was taking so long. When he finally did come out, he couldn't speak to them. Then they realized from his gestures and his silence that he must have seen a vision in the sanctuary. When Zechariah's week of service in the Temple was over, he returned home. Soon afterward his wife, Elizabeth, became pregnant and went into seclusion for five months. "How kind the Lord is!" she exclaimed. "He has taken away my disgrace of having no children."

The last breath of the old covenant, the final prophecy from the book of Malachi. "Look, I'm sending you a prophet before the end of it all, He will turn the hearts of the fathers to their children, and the hearts of the children to their father."
And then silence.
Four hundred years of silence.
It's such a long time to be quiet, a long time to not hear a word from your Creator. No more prophets. Generations

pass with only those stories of old to hold onto. Zechariah knew this way. He accepted living without a fresh word, simply obeying, simply following what he had been told to do. *For Zechariah, it was enough to know that God is.*
And then the lot fell to him to go into the sanctuary, to enter into the holiest of places treading all the way to the altar which stood just before the curtain hanging thick in weight and heavy as a reminder, *DO NOT ENTER*. He would come so very near to the holy, silent God. Zechariah had likely never entered the sanctuary like this before, as it is said there were nearly twenty thousand priests at the time of Christ's birth. *The lot to enter in would only fall to him once.* It was an important day for Zechariah, yet everything he had anticipated **would be interrupted.**
God breaks the four-hundred-year silence through His Angel Gabriel. Zechariah is stunned. He knows who Gabriel is. He's heard the stories of Daniel who fell to his face at the sight of Gabriel walking toward him. And Zechariah is shaken to the core. *Why ME? I'm not a Daniel.* A stunned, shaken, overwhelmed Zechariah is relatable to us. When God bends down into our life and interrupts us with His plan, we are left a holy mess.

"Sell your house and get ready to go to Mongolia." That's what mine sounded like. There is not much to do with such a moment. Ignore it and you've lost the precious invitation into an eternal story. Act on it and you've lost your life as you have come to understand it.

Zechariah experiences something beyond his ability to

accept. God is ending an era; the world is hearing again. Yet here Zechariah notices only one thing, **the obvious.** *I'm old.* And it's this entanglement with the obvious that Gabriel cannot tolerate. In the depths of Zechariah's heart, he wonders, *does God even know me? Does He realize my limitations, my real true physical limitations?* Because we have them, don't we?

    As the pilot instructed the flight attendants to prepare for landing, I had a Zechariah response. Looking out the window at the icy topography of a land I was unqualified and unprepared for, *the obvious felt closer than the holy.* I tried to read my husband Troy's face, but he too was swallowed in thought, perhaps wondering the same thing. *When do we get our super spiritual capes?* I realized moments before the plane touched down on my mission field that I was tragically just, *Shari.* I felt fear. *I'm not the right woman for this.* I'm not a world traveler who longs for the next adventure. I just want my small collection of friends and family around my kitchen table in rural Illinois. I don't even feel impassioned to share the Gospel with the world. *God, do you know whom you have sent?* Fortunately, *unlike Zechariah,* I was left with my words although they could not be understood by most in my new country. I leaned heavy into Jesus that first night on the field. The little apartment that housed us was serenaded by our tears in the weeks following our arrival. If this story was to play out as anything less than a disaster, it would be through the power and divine intervention of a God far greater than I could grasp.

Zechariah *submitted to what had happened to him in the sanctuary*. In forced silence he yielded to the story line God had called him into but perhaps still wondered .... *how*. Reaching back to his roots, he leans heavy on a God that IS. "*Zechariah, Zechariah....*" Elizabeth looks into her husband's tired eyes.

"*I'm pregnant!*"

Engage

Challenge yourself to spend the next 24 hours refusing to focus on the obvious instead asking God to open your eyes to what HE wants you to see about yourself and about others. Write down three things you notice.

Overshadowed
December 3rd

Reading

Luke 1:26-37

In the sixth month of Elizabeth's pregnancy, God sent the angel Gabriel to Nazareth, a village in Galilee, to a virgin named Mary. She was engaged to be married to a man named Joseph, a descendant of King David. Gabriel appeared to her and said, **"Greetings favored woman! The Lord is with you!"** *Confused and disturbed, Mary tried to think what the angel could mean.* **"Don't be afraid, Mary,"** *the angel told her,* **"for** *you have found favor with God! You will conceive and give birth to a son, and you will name him Jesus. He will be very great and will be called the Son of the Most High. The Lord God will give him the throne of his ancestor David. And he will reign over Israel forever; his Kingdom will never end!"*

Mary asked the angel,
"But how can this happen? I am a virgin."
The angel replied,
"The Holy Spirit will come upon you, and the power of the Most High will overshadow you. So, the baby to be born will be holy, and he will be called the Son of God. What's more, your relative Elizabeth has become pregnant in her old age! People used to say she was barren, but she has conceived a son and is now in her sixth month. For the word of God will never fail"

Overshadowed. Sometimes it is the only way isn't it? Sometimes the only way through it is to surrender fully to the Holy Spirit and let God do what is not possible otherwise. Mary, *like Zechariah,* had involuntarily entered into a story line in history that no one would forget. In one brief moment she stepped from obscurity to eminence. She asks questions, good questions, **but she believes.** *The Holy Spirit will overshadow you Mary, that is how it is possible.*

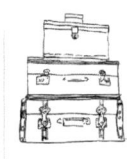

I unpacked our luggage. All twelve pieces had held all we had left in this world, our lives bundled up into these twelve bags. We had moved into our home in the ger district of Mongolia's capital city, Ulaanbaatar, also famous for being the coldest capital of the world. Here in the ger district, there was no running water, no indoor toilet and those early January temperatures were pushing negative fifty degrees. It would have been one thing to be there on my own but I was also mothering four shell shocked children.

Trevor, 15
Sarah, 13
Josiah, 10
Elly 5

As I unpacked our life from those bags, I needed overshadowing. All of us did.

How do we get water, take a bath, buy toilet paper?
What if we get sick?
What if the car won't start?
Who do we call?

Ignorance breeds fear, and I was ignorant. It took great courage to bundle the kids up and walk down the hill to buy a few groceries. It took a fierce release of pride to learn new systems, new words, new manners for everything, *to unlearn a life. Overshadow me Lord ...overshadow me.*

And He did.

I've had moments much further down my road when I grew comfortable and life in the ger district felt possible, when I longed for that overshadowing, the nearness of God, the need for God in my everyday activity because without Him I couldn't move from my fear.

In an effort to pass courage to Mary, Gabriel points to another woman, Elizabeth, and the miracle she too was experiencing. *"People used to say she was barren, but she has conceived a son and is now in her sixth month. For the word of God will never fail"*

People used to say I was fearful.
People used to say I had no self-confidence.
People used to say I was afraid of change.

But after the overshadowing, **they can't say that anymore.** There is something profoundly humbling about having nothing to do with your victory.

Engage

Pray right now to be overshadowed in the areas of your life where you need to see God's victory. In the next 24 hours ask someone if you can pray for them to be overshadowed as well.

Infallible
December 4th

Reading

Luke 1:37

For the word of God will never fail.

Mary, you can trust this. You can trust God in this unexplainable moment. *"For the word of God will never fail."* If He said it, He will do it. Gabriel knows. Gabriel has seen the impossible made possible, many times over.

It was a somber discussion. How would we close down the Desert Rose project? It was the only girl's shelter of its kind in the country. **There were six girls** living inside the shelter and none of them had a solid place to go if the shelter closed. The missionary who had founded Desert Rose was leaving the country and she had no one whom she could pass the torch. Troy and I were established by now. We had built our ministry, planted a church and found our strength in the calling. God had used us despite our weakness, and it had built our confidence in what He could do. We had a close relationship with the founder of Desert Rose and had decided to try to help her solve the logistical problem of ending a ministry. None of us felt good about it. We wondered why God hadn't sent a replacement. The Desert Rose project was complicated. It was run differently than the other shelters in the country and with it came the stresses of trail blazing. Leading the way also meant extra scrutiny by authorities, endless investigations and intensive fund-raising. That night as we closed in prayer, God surprised me again. I felt him speak to me, *"You are going to take Desert Rose."* I knew it was the Lord speaking but it made no logical sense to do what He was saying. I was already fundraising for our own existing project and it was more than enough work for all of us. The feeling became so intense I had to share it with the group immediately as we closed the prayer time.

"God is speaking to me to take Desert Rose." I said.
Even as I spoke it, doubt crept in. I looked around the room to find everyone as surprised as I was. *"Are you sure?"* My

husband Troy asked, realizing more than anyone else the risk of that endeavor. I knew to weigh the call with scripture and it absolutely passed that test. "*Yes, I am.*" I replied.

There were six girls who needed a home, and God was asking me to commit to providing for them. The details were daunting. There wasn't much money in the bank. There was a lot of need and little resource. I began to feel the weight of what I had just agreed to do. Troy had encouraged me as we crawled into bed that night,

"*Shari, if you're going to do this, you have to trust God. Don't worry about the money. If He said do it, He will provide.*"

The next morning when I woke up, I set my mind to trust that God was with me in this, and never look back. Immediately I felt the enemy pounding me with thoughts like, "*You just want to tell others that you run a girl's shelter.*" I knew these were not my own thoughts and they were not from God so I dismissed them. For several days I battled these kinds of insecurities and temptations to walk away from the task.

But then the miracles began.

One day on my way home I noticed a man putting a sign in the window of a beautiful two-story house I had often admired for its regal appearance. The sign said *FOR RENT.* Again, I felt the prodding of the Holy Spirit to stop and tell the man we wanted to rent the home for the girls. As I pulled into the driveway, I knew God wanted our girls here and that He was going to bring us more girls. The house had running water. It was truly luxurious. Even I did not have running water in my home. My excitement grew as I looked around and imagined how it would be full of girls running about. Then, the owner related the costs to me, $3700 deposit. This was ten times the money we had in the bank for Desert Rose, but with hopeful expectation I went ahead and told him we would have the rent in one week. On the way home I told God I was going to trust Him and couldn't wait to see how He solved this problem. It was a first for me to trust this way, the first time so far out of my comfort zone of faith, *but it felt right.* The next morning an email from our home church in the USA informed us they had taken a special collection for our new Desert Rose project. I cried as I read the amount of the donation, without them ever even knowing our need it had come to within dollars of what the owner had quoted me. And this is how the first year proceeded, with God's Word never failing us. There was always food on the table, always shelter and we took in more girls from the street. Each step of faith brought more miracles.

The week of Christmas we were flooded with volunteers from a church in Hong Kong. They brought gifts, games and fast food chicken dinner meals for each of our girls. Everyone was so excited. The Hong Kong team dressed up in the nativity costumes and performed the Christmas story in our Desert Rose Shelter living room. In our daily work we were restricted on what we could share regarding the Gospel so for many of our girls this was the first time they had heard the

Good News of Jesus. Afterward, the girls asked if they could perform for us what they had just seen. The team helped dress the girls in the costumes they had just performed in. We all piled into the living room, turned off the lights and used flashlights to illuminate our little nativity. In all my life I'd never watched a more beautiful rendition of the Bethlehem story. I savored the moment with streams of tears flowing. The girls performed it as if they had soaked in every detail while they watched the first time. *I took it all in.* A room packed with people who biologically didn't belong in the story, and yet they were here fully involved as if these were their own children, cameras out, faces beaming.

"*A Father to the fatherless is God in His holy dwelling.*"
~ Psalm 68:5

And it dawned on me all I could have missed if I had not believed God's Word would never fail. He does what He says he will do. I'm living proof.

Engage

Tell someone in the next 24 hours about God's unfailing word in your life. If you don't know Jesus, ask someone who does to tell you their experience of an infallible God.

Passionate
December 5th

Reading

Genesis 3:15

"And I will put enmity between you and the woman, and between your offspring and hers; he will crush your head, and you will strike his heel."

Isaiah 9:7b

The passionate commitment of the Lord of Heaven's Armies will make this happen!

A promise was made in the garden of Eden, when two lost souls were overcome with guilt and shame. Adam and Eve would be punished, but in the middle of the punishment, a promise, a hint that even then in the mess, God was aware of how He would show up to make it all be RIGHT one day. The image of the serpent's head crushed,
crushed hard,
so hard the heel of the crusher, *a descendant of Adam and Eve,* **bruised.** And God holds to His promises. It's impossible for Him not to. Years go forward and Isaiah reminds the decedents of Adam and Eve that God will make it happen. *How?* By His passionate commitment to His promise. The passionate commitment of the Lord of Heaven's Armies **WILL MAKE IT HAPPEN.** Hold on Israel, The Messiah will come. God is not passively promising, but boldly stating.

I remember a brain storming session with our mission team where we threw out ideas about how to plan for the summer camp we hosted for one hundred orphans from the state run shelter. We could tell when the passion showed up at the table because the conversation turned from what we thought we were capable of doing to what we WANTED to do. Siew Ling, our missionary partner passionate about the plight of the orphan, spoke up,
 "*I want to take all the kids to Disney world....* but I can't

yet....*so I guess I want to bring Disney to them.*
We hesitated for a split second and then gave into the dreams and ideas that were swarming within. Each of us shared how we envisioned creating DISNEY in the country side of Mongolia.

"I'd like a roller coaster for the older kids!" I said.
Hey, we were dreaming so why not. It was fun to dream. After we got all our dreaming out on the table, and realized it was nearly impossible, we decided to go for it.

"Oh it's going to happen." Troy said with a big grin on his face. *"Even the roller coaster."* he added.

Our passion made it happen that year.
All of us got involved, the missionaries, the paid staff, every single one of us invested our time talent and money like a bunch of crazy people. Disney was nearly all we thought of that entire spring. I pray I'll never forget the excitement of the team which may have surpassed even that of the children as we unveiled our makeshift version of the Disney theme park we put together for the children. It came complete with a castle, the Disney characters *(which we all were dressed up like)* and best of all.... a roller coaster. Our passion was bigger than our small budget. It was greater than our limitations and more stubborn than our obstacles. **We did it!**
Sometime during the chaos of that first day, I noted the long line waiting for the roller coaster ride. The kids were all a buzz with how much fun it was. I peeked in to see for myself and found my husband Troy and one of our volunteers hard at work. The roller coaster room was boxed off with sheets,

one of those sheets was the movie screen of a roller coaster ride complete with surround sound roller coaster sound effects. The kids would climb into a swing hung from the rafters of the canopy and Troy and our volunteers would stand behind them pushing them as the roller coaster on the movie screen went up and swinging them down as the movie showed the roller coaster racing down. They would shake the swing and bounce it while the kids screamed as if they were on a real true ride. The guys did this all day long, dripping in sweat, with smiles on their faces.
Passion.

Now dear reader, imagine the Lord of Heaven's Armies. What can stop Him when he is passionately committed? *What or who would dare stand in His way?* And who is the Lord of Heaven's Armies passionate about? YOU.

Engage

What are God's promises to you? Take the next 24 hours choosing to exchange any worry or anxiety for a simple statement, **Our God is a promise keeper.**

Believers
December 6th

Artist, Joanne Thyne

Reading

Luke 1:38

Mary said, "I am the Lord's servant, and I am willing to do whatever he wants. May everything you said come true."
And then the angel disappeared.

Gabriel has just told Mary she was to become pregnant with the Messiah, while remaining a virgin.
Let that sink in for a bit.

I never wrestled with doubt more than when I began to unpacked stories like these for people who had never heard the Gospel before. I observed for the first time what the Bible sounded like to a person who has not spent every Christmas with a nativity in their living room. It is a sketchy sounding story when filtered through that lens. As I unpacked the Bible word for word so that I could explain it well to the unreached, I began to sense the crumbling of so many false beliefs I had gleaned along my Christian walk. There were disturbing things in the Bible that I had never read before. There were things I had believed that were simply not in the Bible. Perhaps I saw a cartoon, or heard a Bible story told that way, and had hung onto it, *a false gospel.* I didn't like the crumbling. I was safe in what I thought I knew about Jesus. Yet, Jesus, the Gospel, the entire message is anything but safe. The Word of God is dangerously transforming to those who will Believe it. But who **would** Believe it?

We never did mean to start a church. It was so accidental it's embarrassing. Accidental is a wonderful word to describe much of what God did with us in Mongolia. Later, we would come home and be interviewed for mission director positions at various churches. We always failed to know the lingo they threw at us*; lingo more polished missionaries would know.* In that world of missions things like planting churches in unreached communities are complicated, blueprinted and strategized. Although I have great respect for that world, *we*

were never in it. For us it began as a knock on our gate, a sweet Mongolian woman introducing herself as our neighbor and asking, *"Will you teach me about your Bible?"*
But we were supposed to spend two years language learning, culture acclimating, figuring out how to do the laundry without running water.... at *least that was what all the missionary books told us to do.* What were we to do with this timeline dilemma? So, we fast forwarded to Bible studies in our living room with a woman we just met. Six weeks into the process with me wresting the tension of how on earth to explain this stuff in a way that doesn't sound like a made-up story, she fell to her knees and cried out to Jesus for forgiveness of sin. *She was our first Believer.* And more followed, *so many more.* Bible study accidentally became a church when neighbors brought uncles and uncles brought friends and friends brought the taxi driver. Some would tell us that they thought we were nuts until Jesus came in a dream to tell them we were right ...He was the one true God and we could be trusted. *Thank you, Jesus, for that helpful, five star recommendation.* Others would come to accept Jesus during worship time, weeping and believing as God revealed HIMSELF to them. One man, came to church for months on end and doubted every time until one day he found himself unable to ask the Buddhist Monk for prayer because he had come to believe the Monk was wrong, there was only one God to pray to...*Troy and Shari's God.* We tried so hard to do it right, to take it slow, to explain it well. We tried to make the Bible stories make sense. But ultimately it had so little to

do with us, our methods and efforts. We missionaries were small, unqualified and prideful. But the Believers believed in Someone greater than us. They believed the story we told despite our flaws because it was the truth, no matter how out of this world it sounded.

Mary, she too believed an absolutely outlandish plan.
"*Okay, I'm willing.*" she responds.
"*May everything you say will happen to me.... happen.*"

So, He {Jesus} said to the Jews who had believed Him, **"If you continue in My word, you are truly My disciples. Then you will know the truth, and the truth will set you free."** John 8:31-32

Engage

Step out of your Comfort zone and ask God to help you tell the Christmas story to someone He directs you to in the next 24 hours.

Noticed
December 7th

Reading

Luke 1:39-56

A few days later Mary hurried to the hill country of Judea, to the town where Zechariah lived. She entered the house and greeted Elizabeth. At the sound of Mary's greeting, Elizabeth's child leaped within her, and Elizabeth was filled with the Holy Spirit. Elizabeth gave a glad cry and exclaimed to Mary, **"God has blessed you above all women, and your child is blessed. Why am I so honored, that the mother of my Lord should visit me? When I heard your greeting, the baby in my womb jumped for you. You are blessed because you believed that the Lord would do what he said."**

Mary's Song of Praise:

Mary responded, "Oh, how my soul praises the Lord. How my spirit rejoices in God my Savior! For He took notice of his lowly servant girl, and from now on all generations will call me blessed. For the Mighty One is holy, and he has done great things for me. He shows mercy from generation to generation to all who fear him. His mighty arm has done tremendous things! He has scattered the proud and haughty ones. He has brought down princes from their throne and exalted the humble. He has filled the hungry with good thing and sent the rich away with empty hands. He has helped his servant Israel and remembered to be merciful. For he made this promise to our ancestors, to Abraham and his children forever."

Mary stayed with Elizabeth about three months and then went back to her own home.

Mary's song. Did you hear it? Her heart is riveted, she is shaken with hope. Listen.

Dietrich Bonhoeffer, a German pastor and theologian who

was executed by the Nazis, called Mary's song: *"the most passionate, the wildest, one might even say the most revolutionary hymn ever sung."*

Mary sings as a woman who knows of the sorrows, hunger, the corruption of government and the disparity between the poor and the rich. **She sings.**

She knows who she is, **and she knows that God has bent down to take notice of her**, *notice of a nation and notice of the world.* You can hear it there, in the song, the tiredness of Mary. She was young but oh so tired of the way the world was going without a Savior.

In the dusty, dried up, riverbed, I felt my stomach twist within me.

It stunk. Everything smelled. The spring sun had thawed the frozen tundra and with it the garbage and the pit toilets of the ger district. It was complicated to get here, to these the slums near the riverbed. There were no real roads and the bottom of our Jeep had scraped against the berm as it climbed over the top to access the area. The family we were looking for was as messy as a mess can be. Broken inside and out. There were two small children who needed help and it was our task of the day to meet them. If I had realized *how difficult that would be, how long of a journey it would take, how desperately entangled my heart would become,* I may not have come at all. Not knowing which ger belonged to them, we walked through the maze of homes calling out their names until finally one little boy no more than three years old waved out to us announcing he was who we were looking for. The sight of him touched a nerve I didn't know I had until that very moment. It was the nerve of injustice. Until now, it had never been meddled with. But it was there, and I discovered it as I looked into the eyes of a filth covered boy. I'd never been near a child so neglected. And then his six-year-old sister came around the corner to stare at me. She was a lost child, as lost as I had ever known. I soon discovered they had been locked outside their home for the day. They did not know where their mom was or when she would return for them. None of this seemed strange to them. It was only I who had to pull my jaw shut and accept the reality in front of me. The two were playing with small rocks turned into a farm by their well-functioning imaginations. The boy showed me his rock horses, rock cows, rock sheep and rock farmer. I pulled out some apples from my bag and the children came for them without an invitation. So did a drunk man standing nearby, who attempted to take them from me before I could give them to the children. Appalled I had the desire to throw the apple at the man's head. Angry, shaken, sickened, I thought, *how is it possible that I have lived my whole life without a hint of suffering while these children, have lived not one day with a hint of wholeness.*

God. God! God do you hear me? Do you see this?
DO YOU NOTICE WHAT IS HAPPENING ON YOUR PLANET? Immediately I began to sense the presence of the Lord. **While I wanted it fixed,** He *was sending me to notice.* I was overwhelmed with the thought that I was the one sent to notice.

There was no one else here besides myself and my missionary partner. Of all the people in all the world it was us. **So now what?** The police were not a safe place at the time. A well-run department of children's services did not yet exist. I thought of taking them home. I imagined myself inviting the children into the car, driving away, ending up in jail that night for kidnapping. The eyes of the people living in this hellish place were certainly glued on me. I suppose they were wondering what I was going to do. Listening to my child-like, Mongolian language I must have been sheer entertainment. *And I too was wondering.... what.... what was I to do?*
"*Let them know you see them.*" I felt the Lord say. "*Let them know you will be back to visit them.*"
That's it? *I wondered.* They finished their apples and we talked about their mom coming home later. I asked them what they liked to do. An irrelevant question for a child in survival mode. *There was no answer.* I told them I'd be back and that I'm thinking of them. They stood and waved at me as I drove up the steep berm. I cried until I threw up.
Noticing felt weak. It felt pointless, *but it wasn't.*
Years went by. Years of noticing these two until I had finally found the way forward. There were many broken visits. Once after a brutal visit where it was obvious the children were in danger, I did try to take them with me, *otherwise known as kidnapping,* but after a bloody lip from the fearful five year old boy crying, "*Just please let me stay here,*" I gave up. I went back to the plan. The original plan that God gave me to see them, to take note of their plight, to enter into their mess and to let them now I am not leaving. And then one day, after all

that waiting, the right doors opened, and God made a way to get them into a home where they were safe, loved, and nurtured. The last I heard of them, they were in school, thriving and excelling. I lost track of them over time and I wonder now if they remember the yellow haired lady who came too often, who once tried to kidnap them, **and who seemed to noticed everything.**

And God came here **to us** *not in a rush, not in a hero's cape.* He took notice of our poor and sick state and came with a long-term plan. He came to us here in our mess as a baby who would grow, grow slow, become one of us. He was noticing from the moment He called out, *'Adam where are you?"* to the manger, all the way to the cross...*noticing.* And It worked. We. Are. Free.

Engage

In the next 24 hours commit to notice what God is noticing. Resist the urge to ignore. Write down three things the Lord leads you to notice.

Loosed
December 8th

Reading

Luke 1:57-66

*Now the time had come for Elizabeth to give birth, and she gave birth to a son. Her neighbors and her relatives heard that the Lord had displayed His great mercy toward her; and they were rejoicing with her. And it happened that on the eighth day they came to circumcise the child, and they were going to call him Zechariah, after his father. But his mother answered and said, **"No indeed; but he shall be called John."** And they said to her, **"There is no one among your relatives who is called by that name."** And they made signs to his father, as to what he wanted him called. And he asked for a tablet and wrote as* *follows, "His name is John."*

And *they were all astonished. And at once his mouth was opened and his tongue loosed, and he began to speak in praise of God. Fear came on all those living around them; and all these matters were being talked about in all the hill country of Judea. All who heard them kept them in mind, saying, "**What then will this child turn out to be?**" For the hand of the Lord was certainly with him.*

It was Elizabeth, who gave Zechariah his words before he could say them. "*NO.*" she speaks up. Everyone looks at her. In Elizabeth's day, it's not appropriate for her to do this, she is so far out of line it's embarrassing. *There are traditions to keep.* The tradition is for Zechariah's son to be named after him, to follow in his footsteps, to become a priest himself. Elizabeth shatters the status quo with her interruption. "**NO.**"
She and Zechariah have had plenty of charade conversations as her belly grew large with John. Elizabeth has read all of what Zechariah wrote regarding Gabriel in the sanctuary. Elizabeth is a follower. She believes her man and she stands by him in this moment. It is thought that Zechariah was also struck deaf by Gabriel so perhaps he is standing in the room next to her, both silent **and in silence.** Elizabeth obeys first when she says, "*Indeed, he shall be called John."* Everyone gets upset. This is not the way it's done. But Elizabeth knows that her little baby boy will not be following his earthly father's

path, instead he will follow his Heavenly Father. She closes her eyes and presses back the tears mixed with fear and joy as the room erupts into a family feud. Elizabeth's statement is dismissed entirely. The guests look to Zechariah. Elizabeth watches her husband as he makes the move that catapults them into a story so much bigger than they could know.

It's Zechariah's turn now. He steps out into obedience as his hand inscribes their son's name on the wax coated writing tablet. He's grown used to communicating this way. He's learned a lot over the last nine months. Foremost, he has learned to listen to God and to obey, immediately. He holds up the tablet so all the befuddled guests can see what he has written. **His name is JOHN.**

Right there, right then in the obedient moment Zechariah's tongue was loosed. "*And he began to speak in praise of God*" By late that evening, *even without social media,* this story was being talked about in all the hill country of Judea. **It was really big news.**

My calling to full time missions came to me when I was a young girl at summer Bible camp. No matter what I did later in life to forget or ignore it, that moment, that call, never did leave me. It followed me through all my choices in life so much that I can remember the feel of the carpet under my knees bowed before the Lord. I knew He was going to send me. But first I sent myself through some heartache, taking the long, lost *and somewhat disastrous* *road to missions.* I married an atheist. That's how far I ran. But when my atheist later came to love Jesus in deeper ways than I had yet experienced, God showed me what was possible even when I had such little faith. For me, it was a loosening that took time. Like a rusted on old metal bolt that has to be taken off, so were my thoughts about myself and others, my lack of belief and my tendency to dwell in fear and worry. Life's circumstances loosened those things off my heart one turn of the hand of God after another until I'd learned to step out in faith and give until it hurt.

A loosening, our child's health fails, I learned to surrender. *A loosening,* I chose to trust God in the middle of the storm. By the time God had called us into full time missionary work in Mongolia we were just about undone, just about loosed enough to be redone. We needed one more act of obedience to get us to the other side, **and it wasn't ours.**

 To say we were close to my mom, dad and sisters is not enough. We spent our days together. The three sisters with coffee and babies running around. Mom and dad were the hub and weekends were spent at their house eating all their food and letting the cousins run wild on the farm. As a family, we were as tight a bolt as you could get. When the entire crew of them followed us to the airport on January 9, 2009 it was an act of obedience to the Lord. By this simple action alone, we felt they were catapulting us out into our next life. *And this is no exaggeration.* It was not easy for them to loose us, but if they had not we may not have been able to stay so long and with such freedom to immerse ourselves in the call. Those last hugs, the tears, the final goodbye was a loosening of such proportion that I could feel it in my soul where something gave way and we were all the way loosed....*free to serve w*holeheartedly, completely, nothing holding us back.

The image of my family waving us forward as we crossed through the security check is burned into my heart partly because of the emotion that's wrapped up in that picture and partly because it was the moment I stepped into the calling. *And how could you forget something like that?*

Engage

Is there someone you need to loosen by lending your support and giving your blessing? If so, make a point today to do what it takes for that person to know you're cheering them on.

Realization
December 9th

Reading

Luke 1:67-77

Then his father, Zechariah, was filled with the Holy Spirit and gave this prophecy: **"Praise the Lord, the God of Israel,** *because he has visited and redeemed his people. He has sent us a mighty Savior from the royal line of his servant David, just as he promised through his holy prophets long ago and from all who hate us. He has been merciful to our ancestors by remembering his sacred covenant— the covenant he swore with an oath to our ancestor Abraham. We have been rescued from our enemies so we can serve God without fear, in holiness and righteousness for as long* *we live. And you, my little son, will be called the prophet of the Most High, because you will prepare the way for the Lord. You will tell his people how to find salvation through forgiveness of their sins. We will be saved from our enemies*

Overwhelmed by the loosening of his tongue, Zechariah sings out the first Gospel message. He gets it.

He knows in his gut what this is all about. After all, he was the one standing there before Gabriel. That pretty much changes everything for a person. He's sold out to the realization that God is here now. God is actively involved again. You can hear the prophecy pushing out from the priest as he sings,

"YOU will tell his people how to find salvation through forgiveness of sins."

You speak the truth Zechariah, forgiveness, all of us forgiven.

The man standing before Troy and I was a liar, a cheat and a thief and he was also our friend. We had worked with him for over a year as he tried with sheer grit to overcome his alcoholism. He didn't have interest in a Savior but politely attended church whenever he was sober. We loved him. This is why it was so heart sickening when we learned that he was stealing from us. Although likely we shouldn't have trusted him given his history with addiction, we chose to give him our belief of the best possible version of himself. After all, a person should never be defined by the worst thing he has ever done. With careful thought to the risk, we placed him in charge of the construction materials needed for the shelter we would build for the street girls. This arrangement went along well **until it didn't.** Things began to go missing and the suspicion led to our friend as the likely culprit. Troy and I prayed about how to respond and God gave us the answer. *Forgive him.*

Yes Lord, we hear you, forgive him and.. *And nothing.* Forgive him. To Troy and I, it felt irresponsible to simply forgive, but in our prayer time the message of the cross frustrated our logic and caused us to slow down and pay attention to the response God was entrusting us to deliver. It had been weeks since we had seen or heard from our thief, so we were surprised to see him arrive to church that Sunday. Directly after the message was over, he asked to speak with us in private. I considered God's words to us, *forgive him.* Forgiveness is very expensive. It's not a simple gift. It can be misunderstood, mis-used, mistaken for weakness. Our thief could not look us in the eye. By nature, he was a reserved and soft-spoken man. But this was the weight of guilt that kept his shoulders bent, head hung low and eyes to the ground. He could barely speak but managed to tell us what we had already deduced, *he was the thief.* "I took and sold so much that I can never pay you back." he said. His voice was pained, his pride crushed. He went on to explain his solution to remedy this was to make payments over the next few years, working for us for free. He never asked for forgiveness but instead expressed his regret and shame. A silence rested between us and his confession. My husband Troy broke the silence with three words. *"I forgive you* The words seemed to have a life of their own as they left Troy's mouth and entered into the thief's sorrow. First he began to shake his head saying, "*No, no no... you can't.*" But Troy interrupted him with, "*Yes I can. God forgave me of my sins, how could I not forgive you."* Then Troy offered another solution suggesting the man continue coming to work as a paid employee but each week replacing something he had stolen. The thief looked up at us for the first time in the conversation. I'll never forget his words, "*No one has ever forgiven me before.*" He then began to weep so hard his shoulders shook, and he cried from a deep place that I had never been invited into. *Years of being the thief, the liar, the cheater the addict ...* all those years cried out. When the tears were over, he stood up and said, "*May I sing you a song?"* It was the oddest response I had ever experienced but of course we said yes. The forgiven sang. The song he sang came from as deep as the cry. Tears streamed as he sang out his gratitude and we stood before him, ourselves overcome by emotion. He got it. He realized that day what it meant to be forgiven. Three words had broken through the fortress of walls he had built to protect his heart. Realization of who God is came with three powerful words, *I forgive you.* **Salvation had come through the forgiveness of sins.**

❋

Engage

Three words, **I forgive you.**
Who needs to hear that from you today?

Tender
December 10th

Reading

Luke 1:78-79

Because of God's tender mercy, the morning light from heaven is about to break upon us, to give light to those who sit in darkness and in the shadow of death, and to guide us to the path of peace.

U**nzipping my tent, I climbed out as quietly as possible.** I was surrounded by the tents of volunteers who had traveled from a collection of countries. The had come from places where there was running water, a hot shower and indoor toilet (*never to be taken for granted*). These were bankers, business owners, doctors, moms and dads, students, an array of souls who had traded their vacation times for *these tents, this week, a hundred orphans or one.* God had interrupted my life and told me to come here to Mongolia. But for these volunteers it was a choice. Most of them had the means to vacation anywhere in the world but instead they chose to spend their time here with the orphans of our city. I was amazed by this decision.

It was cool outside and quiet. I didn't know the time but the last I had looked at my phone it was 11:45pm and many of the volunteers were still singing and laughing inside the community building. Now only darkness. The entire camp slept. I wrapped my sweater tight around me and began the trek to the pit toilets located at the edge of the camp. Once away from the tents, I turned on the flashlight that lit the path before me. It had been a full day. My thoughts drifted to the joy the kids had experienced from all the love of the volunteers. By mid-week the volunteers had settled into a routine and everyone was starting to feel comfortable with the discomfort of communal outdoor living. They were getting so good at '**swimming in awkward**' as I had taught them on orientation day. "*When you jump into ice cold water it's horrible isn't it?*" I had asked. "*And what's the urge right at that moment?"* One volunteer had given the obvious answer, "***To jump right on out!"*** I went on to explain that when you stay in, force yourself to stay, go all the way under and get fully immersed it gets a little warmer. In fact, it often gets so much warmer you don't want to get out. I had finished the orientation with a challenge to all of them, "*Will you swim in awkward this week? Stay in when it doesn't feel comfortable.... stay in and swim around and see what God will do.*"

The kids know the volunteers are coming. They look forward to it. Year after year, the volunteers return. More often, the same ones come back again and again. A family develops without any of us meaning for it to happen. *The night before summer camp* the anticipation runs high for the children. Will **their person** be among the sea of volunteers descending on the camp tomorrow? Just as the volunteers have their favorite kids, **the kids also have their favorite volunteers** and they wait with fingers crossed for them to emerge from the bus. You can imagine the tears when their hopes are not met with reality, and the sheer joy when they are. Regardless, the volunteers that show up *are all in.* Perhaps they were negotiating a multimillion dollar deal the day before they landed in Mongolia, but while they are at the camp *it's all for the kids.* They become kids themselves. Their presence literally changes the atmosphere of the camp. They give every ounce of their heart and soul and because of it, the children are transformed, year after year, from children without families to children **who have** families all over the globe.

    Lost in my task list for the next day I followed the path back to the tents but then something caught my heart, *caught it hard, caught it strong.* The tents all lined up in silence cradled by the most beautiful breathtaking starry night I'd ever seen. The milky way brightly sprawled out in a swirl that

I could reach up and touch in my captured imagination. I stood small and nearly swallowed by God's awe-inspiring handiwork. A fiercely tender and merciful God had made that. Fierce enough to break through heaven and hell to get us. Tender enough to come down for us, **to be all in** as if we were all that mattered.

Looking at the tents lined up like painted pictures under the starry sky that took my breath away, I thought of the act of service, the bending down to come near the orphan, the joy in it. So much like Jesus. So much like Jesus, that it had to be, *Jesus*. I felt the fierce and tender mercy of God in the presence of our sleeping volunteers that night, I felt it as powerful as I felt that night sky. I felt it as if as if God were right near me, *because He was* **in all of them.**

Engage

God's fiercely tender mercy is right near you today. Where do you see it? Don't keep it to yourself, Tell one person about it in the next 24 hours.

Certain
December 11th

Reading

Luke 1:1-4

Many have undertaken to draw up an account of the things that have been fulfilled among us, just as they were handed down to us by those who from the first were eyewitnesses and servants of the word. With this in mind, since I myself have carefully investigated everything from the beginning, I too decided to write an orderly account for you, most excellent Theophilus, so that you may know the certainty of the things you have been taught.

Back to the beginning, back to Luke, *"I too decided to write an orderly account for you,"* For Theophilus, for Believers throughout history bringing us into **today.** Luke writes the story for you and me this Advent. He writes the story differently than his peers, *Mathew, Mark and John.* Luke writes in the detail his mind needs. The details are what's important to Luke. **Certainty.** Luke was not one of the twelve who followed Jesus day to day. He also was not a Jew. Luke, a gentile, *invited in, grafted in, adopted.* He needs to know the story, *the parts that the Jewish people already know* must be learned by Luke. All the details and prophecies are new to him. *"I myself have carefully investigated everything from the beginning."* Luke writes. Perhaps he talks to the twelve, sits with Mary as she pours out all the things hidden in her heart. Luke takes it all in. He stands at the empty tomb and weeps. **What a Savior Luke has found.** And Luke becomes the author of Acts, companion of Paul, inspired missionary, powerful Evangelist. It is Luke's carefully investigated story that we follow through Advent. It is Luke who shares of the journey to Bethlehem, the awe of the shepherds, and God in manger. *"So that you may know the certainty of the things you have been taught."* Luke wants us to know it is not just a story. Luke wants us to know this for certain. If you don't know it for certain, ***you can.*** That my friend, is where the power is.

Our team had spent years living the Gospel with the children at the state run shelter. It wasn't until all those years of loving were laid strong and secure, that we were given the permission **to tell** the Gospel. The telling only came after a long wait. As a ministry team we held to the rules because we loved the kids. Sometimes, we were thrown into the strictly social justice pile by those who would disqualify us as true missions because we were not openly evangelizing. But we trusted the process. Words followed labor, *followed love, followed consistently showing up.* Then one day it was given, the permission to tell the Christmas story. The Christmas party would become our yearly opportunity **to tell God's love,** the story as written by Luke. Thank you, Luke, for writing that story. Your words reach into my generation and touch the hearts of orphans, those carefully investigated words. *Thank you.*

    The second year, the team found a way to share all of what Luke wanted to say **beyond the manger.** Luke the Gentile, Luke the adopted. The theme of the Christmas party was **A Royal Ball.** Each child, **nearly one hundred of them,** was given a royal robe and gold crown. The mood shifted as the volunteers tied the robes on the little boys and girls, fitted the crowns on their heads and told them **how profoundly regal they looked.** The mischievous ones calmed down. The drooped shoulders squared up. The heavy hearts lightened. We could both see and feel change of atmosphere. When all were dressed, the Christmas story was told. All characters were present from tiny baby Jesus to Gabriel, acted out by our enthusiastic team and volunteers. And in the end, it was explained that this baby, He was the King of the world, the Creator of all created things and He had come down for us.

Why? To make us royal. Every single one of us, invited to be royal sons and daughters. Don't think for one moment this was lost on the crowd of orphans hanging onto each word spoken. **It was good news.** The children sat in silence and listened. They embraced the story Luke so longed to be taken for certain. I stood back and breathed in the hope. The hope in those little hearts *that this was not just a story,* and I hoped too, that they would one day know for certain. Amidst the games and treat bags...this was the prize of the night.
Luke's prize...
Luke the adopted, Luke the certain.

Engage

What is one thing you are certain God has done in your life. In the next 24 hours write it down and save it for others to read one day.

Awake
December 12th

Reading

Mathew 1:18-24

This is how Jesus the Messiah was born. His mother, Mary, was engaged to be married to Joseph. But before the marriage took place, while she was still a virgin, she became pregnant through the power of the Holy Spirit. Joseph, to whom she was engaged, was a righteous man and did not want to disgrace her publicly, so he decided to break the engagement quietly. As he considered this, an angel of the Lord appeared to him in a dream. **"Joseph, son of David,"** *the angel said,* **"do not be afraid to take Mary as you wife. For the Child within her was conceived by the Holy Spirit. And she will have a son, and you are to** *name him Jesus, for He will save His people from their sins." All of this occurred to fulfill the Lord's message through his prophet: "Look! The virgin will conceive a child! She will give birth to a son, and they will call him Immanuel, which means 'God is with us.'"*

When Joseph woke up, he did as the angel of the Lord commanded and took Mary as his wife.

We learn from Joseph that even a righteous man must sometimes be disturbed by Angels in order for God's plan to proceed. Mary's story wasn't enough for Joseph. Although he took pity on her feeble attempt to explain away a pregnancy, *they both knew he had nothing to do with.* Joseph had made his plan. A broken engagement, a quiet escape. Perhaps as he closed his eyes with the heaviness of the decisions ahead, he muttered a prayer, "*God be with her....*"

As Joseph drifts into sleep he is forever entered into our nativity sets, the faithful man standing in Mary's shadow. An angel speaks to Joseph's doubt, leaves him with a sense of urgency and a belief that *he too* has been invited into a story too big to understand at the time. "*Don't be afraid to take Mary as your wife.*"

Trust Mary. Trust God.

And he is awake. WIDE awake.

Joseph listens to the sound of his heart beating hard in his chest. A decision to obey what his spirit is screaming means stepping into crazy. No one would recommend he follow through with the next step.

"It's just a dream Joseph, your mind processing the absurd story Mary told you earlier today..."
Yet, Joseph, a righteous man, wakes up and obeys. Mary opens the door in the early morning hours. Joseph stands breathless from the run.

"Let's get married...."

Why did you go to Mongolia?
I often feel sorry for those who ask. I know that what they are about to hear will make them uncomfortable. It makes me uncomfortable too. It is much easier to answer, *"What did you do in Mongolia?"* BUT, why did we go is challenging to put into words without sounding...*crazy*. It's tempting to lighten the story up a bit, so that it falls softer on ears, *to guard our credibility*. By now I'm convinced part of keeping our hearts humble is in the telling of the real answer to that question.

One day, out of the blue, completely *out of the blue,* God spoke to my husband Troy. *"Sell your house and get ready to go to Mongolia."* Troy knew God's voice, knew it was God speaking to his heart, and he was awake. **Wide awake.** God had succeeded in getting Troy's attention. All that you may assume *you might feel* if you had been the receiver of such bizarre instructions, is likely what Troy was feeling too. All the excuses of why this couldn't be happening and all the reasons why he was not qualified were very much alive in his mind. But the moment persisted into the day and was still with him at night. When he woke up the following morning with the same instructions, "**Sell your house and get ready to move to Mongolia.**" Troy decided to obey, asking God, "*Please be the first to tell Shari*" because he really didn't want to be the one to break this absurd news to me. *You know what?* God did that. I was away from home on a trip, not knowing anything God had been speaking to my husband. As I prayed, the Lord spoke to me saying, "*Trust Troy.*" These two moments collided a few days later and we recognized an invitation we had never expected. *An invitation into crazy.* It profoundly moves me to this day, that God was able to convince Troy, **with one powerful sentence,** to uproot his family, *to* walk out of the acceptable boundaries of the American life, to trust God and take a giant step of faith. *But He did.*

    Joseph was a righteous man. But he was simply a man, a human a person. The angel invited Joseph to walk past his own humanity and into an eternal story, but he wasn't given superpowers to do this. When God wakes you up, He leaves you a human, awake. You still have a choice to make from a very human mind. He walks with us. He sends His Holy Spirit to empower us.... **but we must obey.** *Later, even* after all the years in Mongolia, after all the miracles, all the undoing of us, all the places God took us, *we stand awed. How did **that** happen **to us**? How did **we** get to do that?* I find myself looking back at pictures of Troy right before we left for Mongolia like the one attached to this Advent. The photo was taken right after we had purchased our tickets to Mongolia. It was our last vacation as an "*average*" family. Here, he stood on the shore of the ocean, by himself just staring out at the big wide sea. I watched him stand there for some time curious to unlock all the thoughts that must be swirling around in the head of a man who was about to dive into the deepest end of faith.

"*Smile,*" I said, and Troy turned to look at the camera. Right there, *I see it,* the eyes of a man challenged by a mighty, powerful God to go beyond his own capabilities.
I'm so glad he said yes.

Years later, perhaps Joseph went to see the empty tomb for himself when no one else was around. Standing there, his heart pounding in his chest, **wide awake.** He had raised God.

Engage

Consider where God is leading you today, in your home, in your church, in your place of work. Commit to wake up and obey.

Bethlehem
December 13th

Reading

Micha 5:2

*"But you, Bethlehem,
though you are small among the clans of Judah, out of you will
come for me one who will be ruler over Israel, whose origins
are from of old, from ancient times."*

Luke 2:1-5

*About this time Caesar Augusts, the Roman emperor, decreed
that a census should be taken and throughout the nation. (This*

census was taken when Quirinius was governor of Syria) Everyone was required to return to his ancestral home for this registration. And because Joseph was a member of the royal line, he had to go to Bethlehem in Judea, King David's ancient home—journeying from the Galilean village of Nazareth. He took with him Mary, his betrothed, who was obviously pregnant by this time.

Oh, little town of Bethlehem, little town. *You are small among....*
Only three hundred people called Bethlehem 'home' when Joseph and the obviously pregnant Mary came walking up the dusty road. The two, passing by Rachel's tomb as the sun sets low ending the four-day journey from Nazareth. The golden sky lights up the fields once belonging to Boaz, where Ruth gleaned, an unfolding story leading to this very promised moment. Bethlehem, little town where oil dripped from a young boy's head. The City of David. Rich history in such a little town. Rich history and then long periods of silence. *Small, silent town* until today, when Joseph and Mary walk through your gates and you step up again onto center stage. God has a plan little Bethlehem, and in His plans, when His promises are involved, we are powerless.

Often our roads lead us back.
They lead us back to our own Bethlehem where we didn't know we were supposed to be until we arrived at

didn't know we were supposed to be until we arrived at just the right time, in just the right place, for just the right moment.

Shame filled me as we drove away. I would never write home about this moment. Chased to our car by begging children, we drove away in a rush. They had tried to grab my purse, angry boys demanding money, pulling on my arms. I felt afraid but I didn't know why. The worst they would have done is take my bags of groceries, take my purse. *Would that have been so bad?* Hurrying our kids into the jeep and locking the doors, we pushed on the horn to warn the boys and then slowly took off just before they crawled onto the back of the vehicle. *Behind me in the rear-view mirror I saw them shouting in the road.* It was quiet in the car. None of us knew what to say. We had just run away from children. We had run away from the ones we hoped to help. We ran away afraid, ran away angry. Late that night I stood by our window looking out at the dark cold slum. What had I been afraid of? There were too many of them. I couldn't speak the language well. I didn't want to do the wrong thing. *What if* ...
I had been afraid of the what if. So instead of trying to find a solution I had run away. I couldn't shake the sight of the boys yelling in the street. Missionary fail number.... *how many was that now?* I'd lost count. But I too was on a road. A road to my own Bethlehem that was winding, sometimes dangerous, and oh so long to travel. It would lead back to where I needed to be, because as much as I wish to think I am in control of my own life, my own destiny, I am really not, *nor*

have I ever been. I thought of those boys often, imagining the results of a better response. I Learned from them, how I wanted to be. learned from them how fear makes us all the things we don't want to be.*And months fell by the wayside.* Until one night I opened a ger door and stepped into their world again. The ger was dimly lit by candlelight. No electricity and very little heat. As my eyes adjusted to the room, my heart took a giant leap at what sat before me. There they were. The faces I had not forgotten. Three brothers, and one sister who had chopped her hair short and wore her brother's clothing to look like one of them.
"It's safer that way." she later told me.
Earlier that day we had received a call from a local government official. There was a family in dire need, seven children and one dying baby. Could we please go in to check on them? We had dressed warm for the night visit, for it was so cold outside. Up the hill from where I lived, and around just one short corner *was my Bethlehem.* All that time they were living there. How we managed to never bump into one another after that fearful get away in my jeep I will never know, but tonight we were back face to face. A different me, a humbled me, a learner, greeted them. The boys offered me a piece of bread, the only food in the ger. Still now, as I write, I can smell that bread, see it in the warm glow of candle light as the most precious meal I was ever offered.
"We have enough to last us the whole week" the youngest boy proudly announced. *One loaf of bread, a week of meals.*
I asked questions. The children gave answers mostly too

awful to digest. Their parents were garbage pickers, and they were too. None of the children had ever attended school. All were illiterate. They were unregistered, nearly invisible to society. Because of this they couldn't get access to a doctor, or electricity, or solve even the simplest of life's problems. It was going to be a mess to try to help them. Entering into this story would be anything but simple.

"Do you remember me?" I asked the oldest boy, the one whom I last saw in my review mirror, wishing he would say no.

"Yes." the seven-year-old replied.

"Yes, I do."

I went back in my mind, to the jeep for a moment, to a response I'd give anything to redo. And then I silently thanked God for this night, this full circle night, thanked Him for bringing me back to exactly where I needed to be.

Engage

Where is your Bethlehem? Where has God moved all the pieces around for you to walk in at just the right time, exactly as you were supposed to?

Down
December 14th

Artist Elly Tvrdik Age 6

Reading

Philippians 2:1-11

Is there any encouragement from belonging to Christ? Any comfort from his love? Any fellowship together in the Spirit? Are your hearts tender and compassionate? Then make me truly happy by agreeing wholeheartedly with each other, loving one another, and working together with one mind and purpose. Don't be selfish; don't try to impress others. Be humble, thinking of others as better than yourselves. Don't look out only for your ow interests, but take an interest in others, too. You must have the same attitude that Christ Jesus had. Though he was God he did not think of equality with God as something to cling to. Instead, he gave up his divine privileges; he took the humble position of a slave and was born as a human being. When he appeared in human form, he humbled himself in obedience to God and died a criminal's death on a cross. Therefore, God elevated him to the place of highest honor and gave him the name above all other names, that at the name of Jesus every knee should bow, in heaven and on earth and under the earth, and every tongue declare that Jesus Christ is Lord to the glory of God the Father.

I stood outside the nativity scene.
The snow fell soft, the lights from the manger glowed orange and all was silent besides me. The wonder of Christmas has followed me through my life. My parents threw away the commercial aspects of the holiday and left me with raw Christmas. To them, Christmas was a holiday as holy as Easter.
"God came down to us," My mom, *a first- generation believer* told me one Christmas Eve as we had stopped exactly here in front of this same nativity so many years ago.
"One night" she said, "It was over, God had enough of watching us struggle and suffer in our sin. And so, one night, He came to get us Himself."
I was too young to fully embrace what mom was saying then,

but tonight I stood and wept.
I was tired. Mom was gone now. I had come home from Mongolia to meet her at the end of her cancer road. The funeral was over, and it was time to return to the mission. I cried at the nativity for so many things. The years in Mongolia had hurt. They had hurt my heart in ways I may never be able to express. *Poverty, suffering,* they were my everyday experiences. At times I wondered if I could see anything else, anything worse, *and then I would.* In all the ways the mission field had created me, it had also ruined me. I knew had to get on a plane and return to Mongolia in just a few short days. I was disturbed by the sinking feeling in my gut, *I didn't want to go back.* Nearly eight thousand miles between myself and our mission field had numbed the sorrow a bit. *How was I ever again going to willingly enter into that level of misery?* All these thoughts brought me here, back here to this nativity on the side of a country road. I hoped the farmer who put the nativity out each year since my childhood would still have kept with the tradition, and he did. Finding the familiar nativity felt stabilizing in the middle of such inner turmoil. "*I don't know how to do it anymore God."*
Silence.

" *I don't think I have what it takes anymore."* My mind drifted back to standing there by the same nativity with mom. "*Shari,"* she had said, "*Imagine it, that night, that little baby cry.... can you imagine the night God came down...what did that cry sound like?"*
God came down, down to our pain, down to our suffering

down to our mess, to be **with** us. And likely the first thing he did was cry. *One night, it was over.* A baby's cry pierced the air, and it was over. We would never be alone again. I can't imagine a greater act of mercy. I wiped my tears with my coat sleeve and drove home to pack.

Engage

*Where is God calling you to "come down" today?
Will you obey?*

Small
December 15th

Reading

Luke 2:6-7

And while they were there, the time came for her baby to be born. She gave birth to her firstborn son. She wrapped him snugly in strips of cloth and laid him in a manger, because there was no lodging available for them.

A **newborn cry echoes from the small shelter. The cry of a newborn baby, is *there any sound like it?***

Helpless, vulnerable, baby. Mary responds as a mother does, wrapping her baby up tight, warming him.

Joseph watches, wonders, what to do next. *What now?* Small, He started small, came small to us to teach us to see small things as so much more than they are. He needed warming, needed to be wrapped tight, *to be held, to be loved.* He needed parents. Joseph places hay in the manger and Mary places God there. Together they look at the baby. *Right there,* a picture the world will paint a billion times over. And Mary and Joseph have no idea they are living a timeless painting in real time for tonight, they are real people, very much alive, breathing, exhausted, uncertain, new parents, awed by the smallness.

Six years old and braver than any soul I know. She held back the tears she had every right to spill out all over everyone. I sometimes wonder where she cried them. *Where did they fall?*

"I'm only here for a little while" she would tell me. And the season came and went leaving a trail of years behind them.

"My mom is almost done preparing things for me to come home." She would say.

The truth was more than a child should ever know, and for many years she didn't know it, but then one day she learned. Walking down the street she spotted her mom and the brave girl's excitement grew. "*Mom! Mom!*" she called, but even when her mother saw her, heard her cry out, her mother turned the other way. *"She must not have heard me."* the brave girl told the others trying to smooth the truth from her mind. She held back the tears and walked home. When I saw her come through the doors of the Desert Rose shelter, she was fire hot angry. She gave dirty looks and stomped up the stairs. The other girls rolling their eyes, calling her by her well earned nickname, "B*oss*".

The anger burned for weeks and burned red. Then it cooled down. What happened after the cool down is what makes her the bravest girl I know. She began to make plans. *"Teach me English please",* she asked.

"*I'll need to learn English if I'm going to be a good director.*" She went on to tell me of her future. She would study hard, become the smartest girl in her school, learn to read so well that her mother would ask for her one day, because her mother could not read. "*I'll read everything to her and help her*" she told me with confidence, *"and then one day, I'll become a director of something. A real boss who will change things for people,"* she added, *"change things for children like me."*

There is no one who could help children "*like her*"more than this brave girl could, *for* she knows what it is like to need so much, *to hope so much,* to want so much **to be loved.** I suppose the world turns out two kinds of people. The ones who meet needs because of their experiences, and the ones who cause needs because of theirs.

"*I have a lot of things I want to tell people.*" she told me. "That's why I need to be a boss."

I imagined her a grown woman. Grown past the hurt and grown into the solution. A 'real boss' who began as a vulnerable, frail and helpless girl. **That kind of boss could**

lead with an unprecedented love.

Engage

Consider the small beginnings inside of you. Look for one small thing today, that has all the markings of awe in the future

Awe
December 16th

Reading

Isaiah 7:14

*All right then, the Lord himself will give you the sign. Look! The virgin will conceive a child! She will give birth to a son and will call him Immanuel (which means **'God is with us').***

Isaiah 29:14

Therefore, once more I will astound these people with wonder upon wonder the wisdom of the wide will perish, the intelligence of the intelligent will vanish

1 Corinthians 1:19

For it is written:
"I will destroy the wisdom of the wise; the intelligence of the intelligent I will frustrate."

A *pregnant virgin.* If ever there were a sign of all signs, here it was. I can hear the rumblings of the *Israelites* as Isaiah prophesied. His words were
  seven hundred years before
  God
    came
      down.
Two thousand seven hundred years line up before this moment, this day, these words.
And they are still uncomfortable to read.
Look at those ancient words without the nativity in mind.
"All right then, The Lord himself will give you the sign. LOOK! The virgin will conceive a child! She will give birth to a son and will call him Immanuel (which means, God is with us.)"
Does it sound bizarre? It should. It is a sign from the Lord HIMSELF. It **should be** a showstopper. God meant it to be. This was no secret birth, no private hidden away moment, He meant it to cause wonder, to make people shake their heads, to bring the room to quiet. God is about awe. he is about wonder. He does his outrageous work in ways that make the

wise cackle at the absurdity.

" I will astound these people with wonder upon wonder; the wisdom of the wise will perish, the intelligence of the intelligent will vanish."

If the nativity sounds unbelievable to you, it's okay, it was meant to be astonishing. It also means God did exactly what He set out to do. He set out to create a story that could not depend on human wisdom. The ways of God are unlike ours. He out does our wildest imagination. He doesn't stick with our systems and strategies. He remains outside of us *and yet very near us.* As tempting as it is to wrap the nativity up into a snow globe and tell it pretty, tell it in a way that is digestible, pretend that it makes sense.... ***don't.*** Please don't. In doing so, we miss the whole point of our powerful God's sign. He does not expect us to turn off our thinking and pretend His outrageous plan is normal. No indeed, instead, may we revel in the overwhelming, excessive lengths He went through to impress us with this SIGN. Sometimes, the only response to God's unbelievable solutions is to fall on your face and be amazed. Believers, **we do not have to** NOR COULD WE EVER PROPERLY explain our God's ways.

Eight years on the mission field taught me AWE. Without asking for funding we would receive what we needed to the dollar amount. We would receive it from people who didn't even know of our need. Many times over we received. A fire started on a windy night, burned down the fence that was within feet of our

community center. Feet. And yet the community center, sitting vulnerable in the direction of the wind, did not catch fire. Mongolian government officials randomly changed their minds about forcing our nonprofit to pay back taxes *(that we did not owe)*. Thousands of dollars *(that we did not have.)"or else..."* Troy cried out in prayer while the rest of us pulled our hair out and they called back to say, "*Never mind...*" God started a church in an unreached community *using us.* Using a carpenter and a soccer mom.
There are so many other, overqualified humans who could have done that.
But God, **God awes.**
Take comfort in that. Receive comfort in His greatness, comfort in His ability, comfort in His desire to awe you today.

Engage

Where has God awed you? Kneel down. Thank Him for being much more than you can grasp.

You
December 17th

Photo by Dan Hennenfent

Reading

Luke 2:8-12

And there were shepherds living out in the fields nearby, keeping watch over their flocks at night. An angel of the Lord appeared to them, and the glory of the Lord shone around them, and they were terrified. But the angel said to them, "Do not be afraid. I bring you good news that will cause great joy for all the people. Today in the town of David a Savior has been born to you; he is the Messiah, the Lord. This will be a sign to you: You will find a baby wrapped in cloths and lying in a manger."

Shepherds watching their sheep, *warmed by the fire, drifting off to sleep.* As Mary labors in a barn, shepherds breath in the last air of a world without a Savior. This is it. This is the moment God has waited for *and **He is ready to announce it.*** Poor shepherds watching their sheep, drifting off to sleep, they are within moments of being the first to be caught into the embrace of a God so ecstatic He can't contain Himself.

Shepherds, lowly ones, God is coming to you.

A baby's cry pierces the Bethlehem night and Heaven touches earth. Part victory moment, part birth announcement. **TERROR.** The shepherds cover their faces at the sight of God's powerful announcer. The Angel. *Why us? Why me?* Perhaps they are reminded of a secret sin. Has God come to end them? But right here He shows us just how much new we will be experiencing from now on.

"Do not be afraid, I bring you GOOD NEWS, it will cause GREAT JOY." The shepherds are listening. So near to God and yet still living, despite their lowly state, despite their sin. "A *Messiah who is Christ the Lord."* They are invited, and they are wanted. God chooses the lowly shepherds first. "*This will be a sign **to you.** You will find the baby wrapped in* swaddling clothes and lying in a manger." The sign, it turned out, was for the shepherds. Your Messiah is in a manger. He's here now, for YOU. **You** are included. *You,* the uneducated. *You the lowly, you, the poor, you, the insignificant...**No more.***

"I'm going into the Gobi Desert for forty days." Our director Dan Hennenfent from the USA was writing to us with half a request for help, half a baring of a heart.

"*I believe God has told me, 'Meet me in the Gobi Desert for forty days.*" Dan was anything but dramatic. I knew that he was being called to the Gobi, but I wondered why. A year and a half later Dan flew to Mongolia and headed out to the southern borders of the Gobi. I watched him leave our house and wondered how he would survive. We did not hear from Dan for those forty days, and the excitement mounted as we counted down the last of the week before we would drive the fourteen hours to get him. *We did find Dan again, sort of. We found a different version of Dan.* A Dan who had met God, *in a new way.* With his permission I tell a long and lovely story *briefly and simple.* Dan had been invited to live with a family of nomads. Here he met a lowly shepherd insignificant by all the worlds levels of measurement. The Shepherd was poor in material goods and physically handicapped. The Shepherd had befriended Dan. This made things complicated for Dan. He had fully intended on fasting and praying and to '**meet God.**' But the Shepherd was lonely and thankful to have a person nearby, *even if they didn't speak the same language.* He would visit Dan often, bring food, bring games, learn English, observe Dan. Outside Dan's small ger lay the vast sand dunes of the Gobi. One day Dan decided he wanted to climb to the peak. As he packed up his hiking supplies, the Shepherd made motions to Dan indicating he wanted to climb the dunes with him. Dan hesitated. The shepherded had physical handicaps that Dan thought may slow him down. He really wanted that alone time to meet with God. He imagined all that could go wrong on this adventure. Dan's mind said *no* simultaneously with his mouth saying *yes. Dan was prepared for all that could happen but not for what actually did.* The shepherd beat him to the top of the dunes and waited patiently for Dan to catch up. When Dan arrived to the summit the shepherd shouted at the top of his lungs, "**HALLELUJAH!**" Surprised that the shepherd knew that word, *Dan wondered what had just transpired.* Using his index finger, the shepherd drew a cross on the palm of his own hand, He tried to draw pictures in the sand with a stick, but Dan could not make sense of any of it.

Unable to communicate any more than that they walked down the dunes together...*this time as friends.* Something had connected them.

Five weeks later when we pulled up in the jeep to find Dan *thankfully alive,* the shepherd was there too. Dan and the shepherd could hardly wait for us to get settled. They both wanted to know so much from one another. But the shepherd spoke first.

"Once, years ago I went into the city and while there I learned about Jesus. I believed and I followed God for the first time in my life. I joined a church and had a Christian community around me. Eventually I had to return to the desert to help my family. But it was difficult because my family did not *believe and they were angry with me for not being Buddhist like them..... I became so lonely here in the desert. I was told by other Christians before I left for the desert that if I didn't forsake my family and the celebrations of the holiday traditions, I couldn't be a Christian. I didn't believe that and I tried anyway. Finally, the pressures were too strong and realizing I was the only Christian I knew in the entire Gobi Desert, I decided that* **'God must not live in the desert'** *so I decided not to be a Christian any longer.* **And then you came here Dan.** *I COULD NOT BELIEVE IT WHEN I SAW YOU OPEN A BIBLE. I couldn't speak your language or read your Bible but I knew you were a believer. I watched you these forty days and I was so amazed by how you followed God. You were very different from the other Christians I had met in the city. That day I stood on the dunes I shouted,* "**HALLELUJAH**" *thanking God for showing me that* **God was in the desert too.**"

Dan was led by God to a lost shepherd. *Together they each met God in the Gobi.* I cried buckets of tears on that trip home from the Gobi, as Dan expanded on the story of what he had just experienced. I recognized how God is true to His word. He does not leave any of us, *not a single one of us* alone. There is no one, not one, insignificant to Him.

A shepherd cries out alone in the Gobi Desert. A man in his sixties stands in church and hears a call, **"Meet me in the Gobi for forty days."**

FOR UNTO YOU IS BORN THIS DAY.... UNTO you.

Engage

Ask God to show you who you see as insignificant. Ask Him for a heart like His for all people.

Glory
December 18th

Reading

Luke 2:13-14

Suddenly, the angel was joined by a vast host of others—the armies of heaven—praising God and saying, "Glory to God in highest heaven, and peace on earth to those with whom God is pleased."

The shepherds, still on the ground unable to face the angelic being speaking to them. Announcement made. Message delivered. **And. Heaven. Erupts.** *Suddenly.* The armies of heaven praise God together in plain sight of humanity. Can you imagine the power, the force of hope that ran out in that praise? Could anything on this earth compare? *"Peace on earth to those whom God is pleased."*

The shepherds are looking now. How can they not just swallow it all whole? This is happening to them. Perhaps they join the angels in praise. The quiet mountain side is in full revival with a birth announcement like none other. God is not hiding. He never has been. He is breaking open the barrier between His people and heaven. It's a celebration.

And this exact same motive pulled me out of my house on many a Christmas Eve night in Mongolia. Even though it was often below zero in temperature, I could not resist the song. Christmas was not yet fully celebrated in Mongolia which was a post-Soviet nation. Christmas was new to our Christian friends. I could describe Christmas in Mongolia as clean. *Clean, pure, Christmas.* It was all about Jesus, people, hope. The commercialism hadn't hit yet, it was considered a strictly Christian holiday. To celebrate Christmas was equivalent to carrying your Bible into work, it was a statement of faith. Carols were worship songs to the **"one God."** I don't know how the tradition began to go out to homes and sing praises on Christmas Eve, but somehow one of us came up with the plan and the rest of us bravely jumped in. The joy our songs created was contagious. We would visit the hurting, the sick, the hungry, the addicted, the broken family, the poor and suffering and SING THE GOOD NEWS TO THEM. We'd show up in the dark despair, **suddenly,** to show the darkness Who is here now, *Who has the power over death and hell, Who the winner is.* Because as a team, we needed the reminder. We had lived with the sadness of the worst of humanity's suffering. WE saw what evil does to families, to children, to entire communities and it was heavy, too much to bear. Our caroling was our fight back. Depression **meets** joy. Poverty **meets** blessing. Addiction **meets** freedom. A reminder to the enemy of all enemies, **you have been defeated.** And we know it. THE GLORY OF GOD WAS WITH US. On those dark streets, on the coldest Christmas Eves, we were full of the glory of the Lord and it was beautiful. The result of the armies of heaven praising was the world's very first believers. The shepherds would never need to be convince that Jesus was the Messiah. They had seen and heard all they needed to believe.

Engage

Are you fighting darkness, depression, suffering, pain? Join the armies of heaven in praising our God. Fight back with worship today.

Found
December 19th

Reading

Luke 2:13-14

Suddenly, the angel was joined by a vast host of others—the armies of heaven—praising God and saying, "Glory to God in the highest heaven, and peace on earth to those with whom God is please."

When angels leave you, you're never the same. Perhaps you become a little bit ruined for the ordinary. The shepherds were left standing on the ground they once considered as nothing but a grazing spot for their sheep and now it was *oh so holy*. Their words are their first proclamation of faith, *"Let's go to Bethlehem! Let's see this thing that has happened!"*

The angels and heavens armies did not leave skeptics on that holy ground, but rock solid believers. They hurried to small Bethlehem and looked in places where animals were fed. **The sign** was not lost on them, a little baby in a feeding trough. It was just as odd a sign to the first Believers as it would be to us today. **And then they found Him.** *I imagine that moment, the excitement, the awe.* Spilling over, they speak to Mary and Joseph of the night they just experienced, and the words sustain hope in the new parents. They are not alone now in this bizarre ordeal. God has introduced the story to shepherds. The group of them huddle around the baby. There isn't a dry eye. Everyone knows they made history. God chose them all, and no one really knows why.

We have searched many times over for children lost on the streets. Children who were drawn back. Drawn out of the safety we offered them and drawn back to the life they have known on the streets. One small boy struggled so much staying off the streets. "*I don't know why…but it's easier there"* he once told our team. He used words like, familiar, comfortable and friendship. Here in this season, I learned that one can be so familiar with discomfort that it is indeed preferred. As winter approached, one of the team members had a brilliant idea to one of our team members had a brilliant idea to give our runaway a bright orange coat so that the next time he left us all the guess work would be eliminated when trying to identify him from a distance. It worked. Troy and our ministry partner Munkhuu drove the streets in the early morning hours searching for the orange coat boy. They spotted two boys fighting, and in the scuffle, you could clearly see a bright orange coat. Troy drove up next to the dueling pair and Munkhuu opened the car door, scooping him up by the back of his coat and driving off with him. He cried. He did not want to be found.

"Why do you keep finding me!!" he yelled.

He wanted to be where he felt comfortable. Sometimes darkness is comfortable. Being found means entering into a whole new story, an entirely different life. It means overcoming things that are hard to overcome, laying down habits that we may feel we can't live without, being vulnerable in the new thing, being challenged. This boy ran away countless times. We exhausted so many hours looking for him, bringing him back and losing him again. But our team never gave up. There was always enough grace to keep us looking. And then one day, **he stopped running.** He at last believed he was worth a comfortable life. He made the decision to settle into a safe place, find safe friends, and trust the process. That is when we truly found him.

Found him for good.

Engage

Ask yourself if you are looking for God today or if He is looking for you. Are you found?
Have you found the hope of the world?
Meet Him in prayer, before you do anything else.

Tell
December 20th

Reading

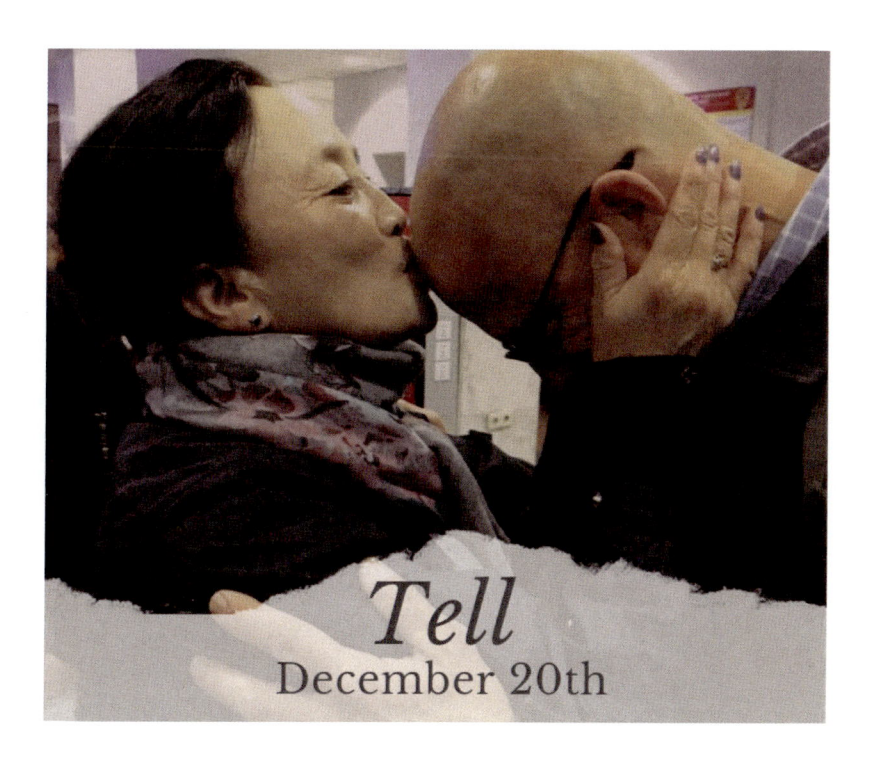

Luke 2:17-18

After seeing him, the shepherds told everyone what had happened and what the angel had said to them about this child. All who heard the shepherds' story were astonished.

Look at your nativity today. Those shepherds, the insignificant place holders, notice them. For these were the first to tell. The first humans to speak it out, to 'go' and share the good news. They can't contain it. The sky had opened up with the armies of heaven. They

91

praised God with Angelic beings. They were the first to find Him, little baby small in a feeding trough, a *"sign to you."* They heard Mary's story and Joseph's encounter. Perhaps this spontaneous gathering in a barn was indeed the very first church. Believers gathered around the manger. But they didn't stay together for long, no, there was work to do. There was a telling to happen. The first missionaries leave the barn door open as they rush out. People have to know. They must know. Everyone must know.

"Please, let's pray for my family." she said. New believer, full of Jesus, faith just hours old. *"I want them to know it like I do, to know there is only one God."* And so together we prayed. We looked toward her house which was just steps from our front door, held up our hands and prayed. She too, came from small things, a simple one room home with a lifetime of financial struggle behind her. But suddenly, it became imperative she give her time and energy to the living and telling of the Good News. I hired her as my translator for half of what she was making at a larger organization. *"Maybe wait until we receive more funding so I can pay you better,"* I suggested.

"I want to do this work," she said, eager to get started. The two of us began what would become years of partnership together in a story only God could write. Months later, at her

baptism her mom stood by my side, invited by her daughter, she came to support what she didn't understand. She was not a believer when she arrived that day, but when her daughter came up out of the water, the Holy Spirit overshadowed the mother and she was never the same again. Together, the two of them began to **go and tell**, **live and tell**, live changed, live free, live God's unconditional love. People were reached. Families were touched. A community was created. In the next round of baptisms Troy asked them to baptize those they had brought to the Faith. "*You are the church*" he said.

Baptize them, stay with them, disciple them, tell them more... keep on telling...

The day we left Mongolia our first Believer's mom kissed Troy on the top of his head saying, "*Thank you. You are the ones who told us. Without you we may have never known about Jesus.*" And **we** may never know how all the telling is still going on today... long after the missionaries have departed or just how far the telling may go.

Engage

Go! Tell someone today. Tell what God has done for you! In the next twenty-four hours make the telling your passion.

Ordinary
December 21st

Reading

Luke 2:20

The shepherds returned, glorifying and praising God for all the things they had heard and seen, which were just as they had been told.

Romans 12:1-2

So here's what I want you to do, God helping you: Take your everyday, ordinary life—your sleeping, eating, going-to-work, and walking-around Life—and place it before God as an offering. Embracing what God does for you is the best thing you

can do for him. Don't become so well-adjusted to your culture that you fit into it without even thinking. Instead, fix your attention on God. You'll be changed from the inside out. Readily recognize what he wants from you, and quickly respond to it. Unlike the culture around you, always dragging you down to its level of immaturity, God brings the best out of you, develops well-formed maturity in you.
~The Message

The shepherds swallowed the extraordinary. Their silent night interrupted, likely forever wrecked them for the ordinary. Still, they went back. They returned to the sheep, to the everyday life, the everyday coming and going life. But they praised God, glorified God for the chance, the opportunity, the invitation to have heard and seen what most never would. When did they finally fall asleep? What did they dream? And when the sun came up, who had they become?

I write this Advent from a warm house in the prettiest part of Illinois. I'm surrounded by nature. A big picture window that frames a forest full of trees covered in white from last night's snowfall. I already did a load of laundry and it's only 6 a.m. I pushed a button and water came flowing out to wash my clothes. Perhaps not too extra-ordinary for you, *but for me,* three years post Mongolia, *I still get goosebumps!* I wonder when it will get old, the appreciation for water, warmth and cheese? Apart from the superficial into deeper wonders I wonder when I will close my eyes to fall asleep and not see the faces of unloved children?

Sometimes, in a room full of friends, I am deeply lonely. I don't know what I'm lonely for. *Is it for a people? A place? Is it for the thick coal smoke? Am I lonely for suffering?* Wouldn't that be so odd? Perhaps I am lonely for the extraordinary. A lonely for a constant clinging kind of dependence on God. A lonely for the years I spent in celebration of what I saw and heard. Because what we saw and heard on the mission field was so worth celebrating. And here now, who am I when the sun comes up? *Who am I with running water, warmth, provision?* **Who am I in the ordinary?** *May I be as the shepherds on the hill,* surrounding the morning fire, warming their hands, stretching the night kinks from their bodies as the sun rises on the first day, the first day of ordinary, *after they have seen so much more.* May I too choose to glorify and praise God for all the things I have seen and heard. May I remember, in the mundane and live what I was so privileged to be a part of.

Engage

Write down two words, two words describing what you may be lonely for today. Ask God to fill those lonely places with a desire instead to glorify and praise Him today.

Seek
December 22nd

Reading

Numbers 24:17

*I see him, but not here and now.
I perceive him, but far in the distant future. A star will rise from Jacob; a scepter will emerge from Israel. It will crush the heads of Moab's people, cracking the skulls of the people of Sheth.*

Mathew 2:1-8

After Jesus was born in Bethlehem in Judea, during the time of

King Herod, Magi from the east came to Jerusalem and asked,

"Where is the one who has been born king of the Jews? We saw his star when it rose and have come to worship him."

When King Herod heard this he was disturbed, and all Jerusalem with him. When he had called together all the people's chief priests and teachers of the law, he asked them where the Messiah was to be born. ***"In Bethlehem in Judea,"*** *they replied,* ***"for this is what the prophet has written:***

"'But you, Bethlehem, in the land of Judah, are by no means least among the rulers of Judah; for out of you will come a ruler who will shepherd my people Israel."
Then Herod called the Magi secretly and found out from them the exact time the star had appeared. He sent them to Bethlehem and said, "Go and search carefully for the child. As soon as you find him, report to me, so that I too may go and worship him."

Long before the Magi *there was Balaam.* For almost everything positive, *there is a counter negative.* For Israel, there was Moses. *For Midian,* there was Balaam. The Middianites needed to end Israel and since Balak, the King of Middian was aware that Israel was obviously led by the supernatural so he strategic-ally chose to fight them at their own game. Balak hired the great and powerful prophet Balaam to curse Israel. Balaam was on his way to bestow the curse of all curses when he was stopped by a sword wielding angel. Falling on his face in a come to Jesus moment *long before Jesus,* Balaam asks for permission to return home...*alive.* The angel informs Balaam that he won't be going home until Balaam speaks every last word that God has designated for him to speak. What follows is a blessing instead of a curse. Tremendous blessing on Israel. Overflowing blessings and prophecy of blessings on Balaam's enemy Israel uncontrollably fall from his mouth.

And here is where we first meet the famous star of Bethlehem. Balaam speaks:

"I see him, but not here and now. I perceive him, but far in the distant future. A star will rise from Jacob; a scepter will emerge from Israel. It will crush the heads of Moab's people, cracking the skulls of the people of Sheth."

Many years follow, bringing us to the Magi, wise men, astronomers, *the seekers. They were* likely from the same area in Persia where Balaam practiced his sorcery and passed it down from generation to generation. Poor Balaam had lived through quite an ordeal all those years ago. How would he have not told of his epic face off with the God of Israel, and a power that overshadowed his very mouth. It was a story that endured. And as generations passed, **all seekers** knew the time was getting closer and closer to Balaam's *"distant future."* The Magi knew of Balaam's prophecy and of what Balaam *"saw".* They knew the king would be coming. They understood a star would be their sign. They were seekers of what Balaam prophesied and when they recognized it was finally coming true *the seekers had to worship, just as Balaam* *had to speak blessings.* And so they came from the East in great anticipation, in full knowledge that they were the ones who understood what was truly happening to Israel, even when Israel's King ***did not.***

The night had been packed with Christmas cheer, *games, food, gifts and music.* It was a party for teenagers, but all of our adult team were warmly accepted despite our very low 'cool' factor. The center we met in was a type of holding place for children too old to be in the orphanage and yet too unprepared to be in the **'real world.' *These were orphans grown.*** Emerging adults, but still without family still without a home. I often thought this must be the worst kind of orphan to be. *Who would take pity on a boy nineteen?* Who would see past his anger and rough exterior and straight into a heart that cried for a dad to call him 'son' or a mom to call him loved, ***just once.*** ?

It was a sad and mournful shelter built by a government who didn't know what else to do with these aged-out orphans. They had one or two short years here, *and then it would be time to fly.* But where? To who? If ever there were a place I could feel the suffering it was in this shelter. Heavy hearts walked these halls, *but they were overcomers as well.* Despite the heavy, they endured. The Christmas party was a time to pause the stress of survival, to eat well, play games and have fun. Our ministry partner, *who was called to enter in and love these young people,* chose a different way to close off our evening of fun. In truth, it may have become my most treasured memory of all Christmas memories in Mongolia. We turned off the music and circled up. Each person was given a candle. The first candle was lit and then the flames were shared until the entire circle was shining. Our ministry partner spoke up. She talked about hope. She spoke of quieting our hearts and listening, of seeking to hear what our hearts really wanted to say about our own pain from the year, about our mistakes, our grief. She told us all how valuable it was to forgive, to forgive ourselves if necessary and to forgive others.

"It's important," she said. "**To leave it here if possible, and to not take it into the next year"** into our next decisions, into our next relationships.
She told us we would all be silent now and that when we found our answers, when we were ready to leave it behind us we could blow out our candles. The lights went off, leaving us all in the glow of our candle. You could feel the silence thick, and it lingered for long. No one blew out their candle. The orange light glowed while they began to seek, *and seek, and seek.* As the silence stayed, the atmosphere in the room changed. Authentic hope came with the seeking. You could feel that too, the letting go of failure, disappointment, and shame, the forgiving. And after a long beautiful while, the first candle was blown out. *But no one rushed.* They kept seeking inside their hearts until they knew it was time and slowly candles were blown dark one by one until there was but one more remaining candlelight. *And we all waited.* We silently cheered him on in his seeking, such big work taking

place in silence. Letting go is big work. Wrestling with hurt for so long can leave you exhausted, but forgiveness is risky. Forgiveness is brave. The love in the room was heavy like it should be for all in this life, for all who are looking for hope, forgiveness, a new beginning.

And soon the room was dark .

Engage

Seek. Spend some time right now to listen to God's still small voice. When you find what you need to leave with Him, thank Him for the gift of new beginnings.

Gifts
December 23rd

Reading

Mathew 2:9-12

After they had heard the king, they went on their way, and the star they had seen when it rose went ahead of them until it stopped over the place where the child was. When they saw the star, they were overjoyed. On coming to the house, they saw the child with his mother Mary, and they bowed down and worshiped him. Then they opened their treasures and presented him with gifts of gold, frankincense and myrrh. And having been warned in a dream not to go back to Herod, they returned to their country by another route.

Overjoyed, they had not lost their way. *The seekers were now travelers, adventurers, risk takers* and they were overjoyed when they saw again, the star, His star. The sign to those who were looking.

Mary opens the door to foreigners, men, speaking another language, rugged from a journey, smelling like camels. **They know who she is,** the mother of a promised Redeemer. The Redeemer toddles around the room, while Mary puts the breakables out of reach, and the wise men are face to face with a prophecy thirteen hundred years old. They are awed. **They bow to him.** Mary doesn't understand their words, but their actions speak. They know. Again, she revisits the night of her birthing in a barn. She lets the memories come forward of the breathless shepherds she will never forget, the things they told her they had seen, their excitement.

It's happening again, a reminder that the sleepless nights nursing, the frustrated days with a toddler, they are simply temporary, all leading to a divine moment of which she still is uncertain of the ending.... **where will this end?**

The foreigners give her little boy gold, frankincense, myrrh and the expense is staggering to Mary. The blessing. The tremendous blessing laid down as gifts for her child. As the foreigners place their luxurious gifts at her boy's feet they look up to catch her eyes filled with tears, hands trembling she nods.

Our church had grown to twenty.
Twenty people from our community. Some had heard of Jesus for the very first-time right there in

our living room. **He had come to get them,** He *found them in the ger district slums, He saw them picking garbage, He noticed them fighting addiction, He saw their cry in the orphanage, and he showed up to transform. When they found Jesus **they too** were overjoyed. The fruit of their joy was to give.*
"Why don't we take offerings here at your church like they do at other churches?" one of our first believers asked.
I went on to explain that we are not really an official church. Troy wasn't paid to pastor and we didn't need any help keeping the electricity on. She heard what I didn't say.
We don't take an offering because YOU ARE THE POOR, YOU ARE THE SUFFERING. How could we ever take an offering from the poor and suffering?
But she persisted.
"I think we should give something. God has been good to us. He has shown us who He is. That makes me want to give, it makes me want to be good to others."
Troy and I insisted they use their money to feed their families. Most of them made an average of $100 a month with the cost of living equivalent to that in the USA, it was impossible to imagine taking a church offering. One week later she surprised us. *"I've made an offering bag."* She held out a hand sown bag with draw strings to pull it tightly closed. She silenced my resistance with one sentence. *"Even the poorest of us has something to give."* she continued: *"I'm going to leave it here on the shelf. If anyone has anything left to give, or if God tells you to give, please put it into this bag and we will see what God will do with the money of the poor."*

was speechless as the room erupted with clapping. They were overjoyed to consider giving. As the months passed by, I would see occasionally, someone excitedly slipping money into the bag. Everyone looked forward to taking part in filling that bag. We never moved it. It sat for six months in the same spot. One day, while dusting the shelf, I noticed the weight of the offering bag.

"*Troy,*" I called. "*Are you putting money in the offering?*"
He told me if he had, it was a very small amount. I pulled open the strings to find the bag overflowing with cash. Overflowing with the gift of the suffering poor.
"*Unbelievable.*" Troy said.
That next Sunday we shared the amount with the full group. The house was a buzz with excitement. We prayed over the money, asking God to show us who needed it and how we as a church could help. **Truth is**, everyone in that room needed it. Needed it bad. Not for wants but for survival type needs. And yet they prayed earnestly for God to show them someone in a worse kind of suffering than they were. *And he did.* A woman down the street was very sick and needed medicine. There was no money for her to purchase it and she sat in her home without a way out of her pain and illness. It was quickly decided we were to purchase her medicine and pay her doctor bills. I have never seen a group so excited to meet a need. I felt total shame that I had underestimated their love. I had underestimated their ability to help, considering them helpless. **Helpless they were not. To one woman down the street, they were her rescuers.** Rescued by the

suffering poor. Yes, indeed I too was rescued by the suffering poor. I was rescued from selfishness and stingy giving, from them I learned to give until it hurts. What a gift.

Engage

Give extravagantly today. Time, money, attention, love, whatever you meant to give, give a little bit more.

Keeper
December 24th

Reading

Jude 24-25

Now all glory to God, who is able to keep you from falling away and will bring you with great joy into his glorious presence without a single fault. All glory to him who alone is God, our Savior through Jesus Christ our Lord. All glory, majesty, power, and authority are his before all time, and in the present, and beyond all time! Amen.

Luke 2:19

But Mary kept all these things in her heart and thought about them often.

Psalm 56:8
You keep track of all my sorrows. You have collected all my tears in your bottle.

You have recorded each one in your book.

Mary kept it all.
All the pieces of her heart which sometimes felt held together by a thread, a*ll the questions, all the fears,* she kept the story. She *kept the feeling, kept the moments, kept the shepherds, kept the foreigners* and thought of them often. Mary, overshadowed, was aware of her interrupted story more than anyone else. She tried to have small talk with friends, to enter into their world, but her heart was wrecked for the Divine. She had encountered Gabriel, gave birth to the Messiah, received surprised visits by Kings, she was ruined for ordinary things, **but perhaps she hid it well.** She pondered all these things and kept them close.

I remember everything.
My heart has kept the evidence of a life overseas.

It brings my collection out when I'm least expecting it, spreading it before me when I wish to forget. *Pondering heart, you surprise me.* The small things are kept more than the programs and the ministries. The small things kept closer than the newsworthy events that bring accolade and donations. The small things are what ruined and transformed me. The voice of an orphan boy calling, "*Shari, Shari!*"

It echoes into my nights sometimes.

The conversation in the bathroom while a couple of orphan girls wash their own socks and talk like little ladies, *Small, delicate,* children washing socks because there is no mother to wash for them. The eyes of a sick baby who has come to the end of his life because there was no money at home to send him to the hospital. I arrived too late, *with cash in hand,* too late. The cry of a street boy as he tries desperately to steal clumps of coal from a coal truck, loaded up to deliver to families who could afford it. Hands black with soot, clothing dark from not washing, his cry when the truck pulled away...*the cry of despair.* His family would remain cold.

Those small unwanted details visit me. They follow me into stores where I see things I wish I owned. They haunt me in buffets piled with food. They are there always and maybe forever. Forever to remind me, Shari, you have seen more. To whom much is given, much is required.

I am a keeper, **but so is God.**

He keeps the sorrow of the suffering poor. He keeps track of their tears, and He keeps me. He is able to keep me.

Jesus, Jesus the baby, Jesus the redeemer, Jesus the promised Messiah, is able to keep me, and all those I have loved and cried for. He is able to keep you too. *Your pain, your disappointment, your failure, your loved one, your grief.*

This is the hope of the nativity. The story was only beginning there. When the shepherds left, and the wise men waved goodbye, when angels retreated to a heavenly realm, and the star burned cold, when all faded away into history and the curtain closed on a promised night, ***Jesus did not.***

Look at that baby's face, the tiny one in the manger. Sent down to us, but not for a pretty Christmas decoration. Sent down to us for a day down the road, down the Calvary road. A newborn cry was act one. This was one baby here, to save the world. *Act two would crush a serpent's head,* crush it hard. We must not forget the power of a bruised heel. Because of that, today, this day, the day before our Merry Christmas, *be assured,* the Keeper of all things, keeps you.

Engage

Write down the hope you have right now. Put it in a safe place to find when Christmas is long behind you.

EPILOGUE

They pile into our home early as the sun rises on the icy streets of the ger district. Volunteers who had come to serve the orphanage children. Strangers, most of them, visiting from other parts of the world. My heart sinks as I consider traditions past, traditions my children will never know because in this place, *Christmas looks so different.* I consider how our family back home will gather close, will celebrate without us once again. Perhaps God hears my complaint on what should be a day of victory, perhaps He considers where I came from and perhaps He cares deeply for this selfish heart of mine. One of our new friends pulls out a Christmas cake shaped and decorated into a yule log, another guest a ham with honey glaze that came from Hong Kong just hours ago. *"I can't believe it made it through customs"* she says laughing about the ham transported in her carry on luggage. I can hardly believe my eyes as someone else presents ginger bread cookies with white icing just like I remember from home. *"We love your family, and wanted to surprise you today!"* she says. The house is abuzz with life, laughter, and smells that bring home a little closer. These beautiful people, God's people, God's provision to a missionary selfish and nostalgic. I recognize these strangers as family, as brothers and sisters alive in Christ.

 *"It's okay if it doesn't look like what you think it should, it's who lies inside that really matters....**one baby for the entire world.**"*

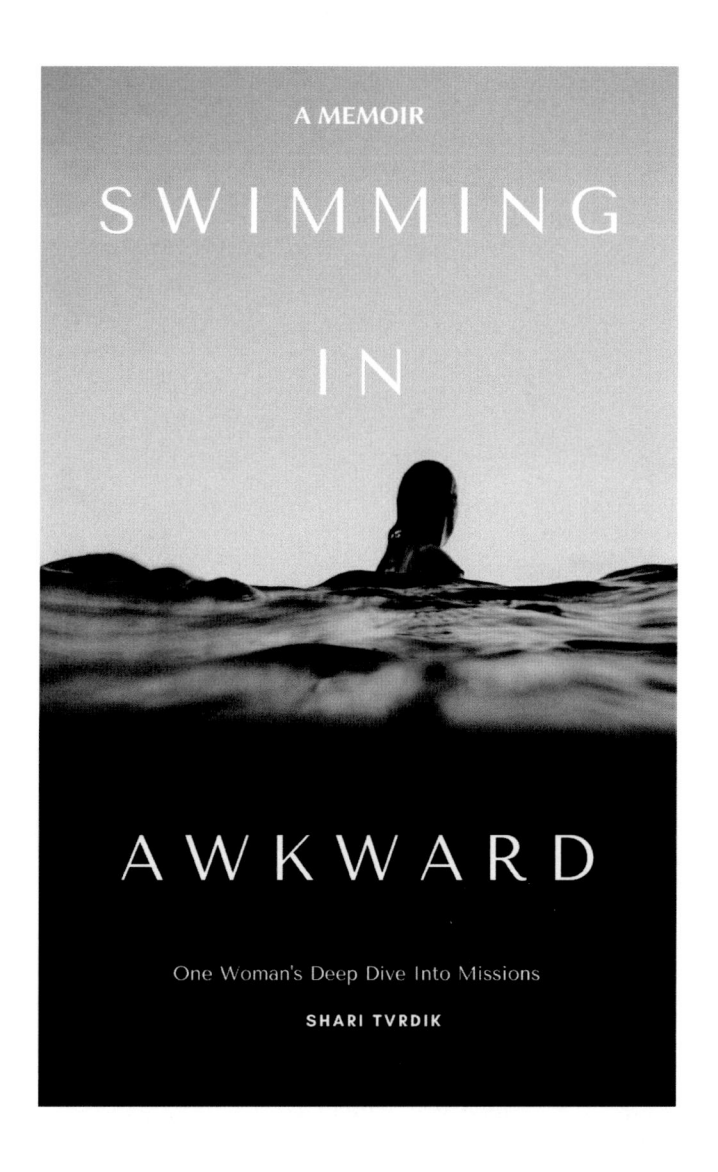

COMING SOON! Read Shari Tvrdik's missionary memoir, *Swimming In Awkward,* the story of one woman's deep dive into missions. Shari invites readers into the true story of a life ruined and rebuilt by missions.

www.swimminginawkward.com

Made in the USA
Columbia, SC
03 November 2023

98defa4f-7316-4287-a751-be0f4a5e5ea6R04